Who Was?
MAD LIBS

by Paula K. Manzanero

Mad Libs
An Imprint of Penguin Random House

MAD LIBS
Penguin Young Readers Group
An Imprint of Penguin Random House LLC

Concept created by Roger Price & Leonard Stern

WHO HQ & Design is a registered trademark of Penguin Random House LLC.

Who Was Albert Einstein? art on cover and interior by Nancy Harrison

Published by Mad Libs,
an imprint of Penguin Random House LLC.
345 Hudson Street, New York, New York 10014.
Printed in the USA.

The publisher does not have any control over and does not assume any responsibility for author or third-party websites or their content.

ISBN 9780843183672
5 7 9 10 8 6

MAD LIBS

INSTRUCTIONS

MAD LIBS® is a game for people who don't like games! It can be played by one, two, three, four, or forty.

• RIDICULOUSLY SIMPLE DIRECTIONS

In this tablet you will find stories containing blank spaces where words are left out. One player, the READER, selects one of these stories. The READER does not tell anyone what the story is about. Instead, he/she asks the other players, the WRITERS, to give him/her words. These words are used to fill in the blank spaces in the story.

• TO PLAY

The READER asks each WRITER in turn to call out a word—an adjective or a noun or whatever the space calls for—and uses them to fill in the blank spaces in the story. The result is a MAD LIBS® game.

When the READER then reads the completed MAD LIBS® game to the other players, they will discover that they have written a story that is fantastic, screamingly funny, shocking, silly, crazy, or just plain dumb—depending upon which words each WRITER called out.

• EXAMPLE (*Before* and *After*)

" _____ !" he said _____
        EXCLAMATION   ADVERB

as he jumped into his convertible _____ and
                                          NOUN

drove off with his _____ wife.
                          ADJECTIVE

" _____OUCH_____ !" he said _____STUPIDLY_____
        EXCLAMATION   ADVERB

as he jumped into his convertible _____CAT_____ and
                                          NOUN

drove off with his _____BRAVE_____ wife.
                          ADJECTIVE

MAD LIBS®
QUICK REVIEW

In case you have forgotten what adjectives, adverbs, nouns, and verbs are, here is a quick review:

An ADJECTIVE describes something or somebody. *Lumpy*, *soft*, *ugly*, *messy*, and *short* are adjectives.

An ADVERB tells how something is done. It modifies a verb and usually ends in "ly." *Modestly*, *stupidly*, *greedily*, and *carefully* are adverbs.

A NOUN is the name of a person, place, or thing. *Sidewalk*, *umbrella*, *bridle*, *bathtub*, and *nose* are nouns.

A VERB is an action word. *Run*, *pitch*, *jump*, and *swim* are verbs. Put the verbs in past tense if the directions say PAST TENSE. *Ran*, *pitched*, *jumped*, and *swam* are verbs in the past tense.

When we ask for A PLACE, we mean any sort of place: a country or city (*Spain*, *Cleveland*) or a room (*bathroom*, *kitchen*).

An EXCLAMATION or SILLY WORD is any sort of funny sound, gasp, grunt, or outcry, like *Wow!*, *Ouch!*, *Whomp!*, *Ick!*, and *Gadzooks!*

When we ask for specific words, like a NUMBER, a COLOR, an ANIMAL, or a PART OF THE BODY, we mean a word that is one of those things, like *seven*, *blue*, *horse*, or *head*.

When we ask for a PLURAL, it means more than one. For example, *cat* pluralized is *cats*.

MAD LIBS® is fun to play with friends, but you can also play it by yourself! To begin with, DO NOT look at the story on the page below. Fill in the blanks on this page with the words called for. Then, using the words you have selected, fill in the blank spaces in the story.

Now you've created your own hilarious MAD LIBS® game!

BRUCE LEE VS. STAN LEE

ADJECTIVE _____

NOUN _____

ADJECTIVE _____

PLURAL NOUN _____

ADJECTIVE _____

NOUN _____

PLURAL NOUN _____

NOUN _____

VERB _____

PART OF THE BODY _____

NOUN _____

ADJECTIVE _____

NOUN _____

VERB _____

PLURAL NOUN _____

ADJECTIVE _____

NOUN _____

NOUN _____

MAD LIBS®

BRUCE LEE VS. STAN LEE

Bruce Lee was the son of a/an _____ opera star. He was an
                                    ADJECTIVE

action _____ and one of the most _____ martial arts
            NOUN   ADJECTIVE

_____ of all time. Bruce once starred in a/an _____
PLURAL NOUN   ADJECTIVE

show called *The Green* _____. His most popular movies are
                              NOUN

_____ *of Fury, The Way of the* _____, and
PLURAL NOUN   NOUN

_____ *the Dragon.*
      VERB

On the other _____, Stan Lee is the _____ of some of
              PART OF THE BODY   NOUN

the most _____ superheroes of all _____. He helped
              ADJECTIVE   NOUN

_____ many of the _____ for Marvel Comics,
      VERB   PLURAL NOUN

including _____ Man, _____-Man, and
              ADJECTIVE   NOUN

_____.
      NOUN

MAD LIBS® is fun to play with friends, but you can also play it by yourself! To begin with, DO NOT look at the story on the page below. Fill in the blanks on this page with the words called for. Then, using the words you have selected, fill in the blank spaces in the story.

Now you've created your own hilarious MAD LIBS® game!

MAD LIBS
BY ANY OTHER NAME

FIRST NAME (MALE) _____

A PLACE _____

ADJECTIVE _____

NOUN _____

NUMBER _____

A PLACE _____

NOUN _____

PLURAL NOUN _____

ADJECTIVE _____

ADVERB _____

ADJECTIVE _____

NOUN _____

FIRST NAME (FEMALE) _____

ADJECTIVE _____

VERB ENDING IN "ING" _____

ADJECTIVE _____

PERSON IN ROOM (FEMALE) _____

NOUN _____

MAD☺LIBS®
MAD LIBS
BY ANY OTHER NAME

_____ Shakespeare was born in (the) _____
FIRST NAME (MALE)   A PLACE

in England around the year 1564. He is considered to be the most

_____ playwright of all _____. *The* _____
ADJECTIVE   NOUN   NUMBER

Gentlemen of (the) _____ was his first _____. He
                        A PLACE   NOUN

wrote many plays about English _____ and
                                    PLURAL NOUN

_____ wars. He is _____ famous for writing a/an
ADJECTIVE   ADVERB

_____ _____ called *Romeo and* _____
ADJECTIVE   NOUN   FIRST NAME (FEMALE)

that contained the line "_____ night, good night!
                            ADJECTIVE

_____ is such _____ sorrow, that
VERB ENDING IN "ING"   ADJECTIVE

_____ shall say good night till it be _____."
PERSON IN ROOM (FEMALE)   NOUN

MAD LIBS® is fun to play with friends, but you can also play it by yourself! To begin with, DO NOT look at the story on the page below. Fill in the blanks on this page with the words called for. Then, using the words you have selected, fill in the blank spaces in the story.

Now you've created your own hilarious MAD LIBS® game!

GEORGE LUCAS AND STEVEN SPIELBERG

NOUN _____

PLURAL NOUN _____

NUMBER _____

ADJECTIVE _____

OCCUPATION (PLURAL) _____

NOUN _____

PLURAL NOUN _____

ADJECTIVE _____

ADJECTIVE _____

COLOR _____

PLURAL NOUN _____

A PLACE _____

PLURAL NOUN _____

ADJECTIVE _____

CELEBRITY (MALE) _____

NUMBER _____

A PLACE _____

MAD LIBS®
GEORGE LUCAS
AND STEVEN SPIELBERG

A long time ago in a/an _____ far, far away, two _____
NOUN   PLURAL NOUN

became friends. Together, George Lucas and Steven Spielberg are

_____ of the most _____ film
NUMBER   ADJECTIVE

_____ of all time. George Lucas is, of course, the
OCCUPATION (PLURAL)

_____ of *Star* _____. Steven Spielberg became
NOUN   PLURAL NOUN

_____ in 1975 after directing *Jaws*, a movie about a/an
ADJECTIVE

_____ _____ shark! The two _____
ADJECTIVE   COLOR   PLURAL NOUN

worked together to create the story of _____ Jones, who
                                         A PLACE

appeared for the first time in _____ *of the* _____
                                PLURAL NOUN   ADJECTIVE

Ark. _____ is the star of all _____ _____ Jones
       CELEBRITY (MALE)   NUMBER   A PLACE

movies.

MAD LIBS® is fun to play with friends, but you can also play it by yourself! To begin with, DO NOT look at the story on the page below. Fill in the blanks on this page with the words called for. Then, using the words you have selected, fill in the blank spaces in the story.

Now you've created your own hilarious MAD LIBS® game!

CHOCOLATE TOWN, USA

ADJECTIVE _____

ADJECTIVE _____

VERB (PAST TENSE) _____

TYPE OF FOOD _____

NOUN _____

TYPE OF FOOD _____

ADJECTIVE _____

NUMBER _____

ADVERB _____

TYPE OF FOOD _____

NOUN _____

ADJECTIVE _____

PLURAL NOUN _____

ADJECTIVE _____

NUMBER _____

PLURAL NOUN _____

PLURAL NOUN _____

MAD LIBS

CHOCOLATE TOWN, USA

Welcome to _____ Town, USA! This _____ town
     ADJECTIVE   ADJECTIVE

was founded by Milton Hershey when he _____ a/an
              VERB (PAST TENSE)

_____ factory in the early 1900s. After a while, Hershey,
TYPE OF FOOD

Pennsylvania, became known as "the sweetest _____ on
                 NOUN

earth." That's because Milton had discovered how to make milk

_____ that was sweet, _____, and that would
 TYPE OF FOOD   ADJECTIVE

cost only _____ cents a gallon. The town became _____
    NUMBER   ADVERB

famous for its _____! The streets are named after chocolate,
     TYPE OF FOOD

with the main intersection being Chocolate _____ and
                 NOUN

_____ Avenue. The town's streetlights are even shaped like
 ADJECTIVE

Hershey _____. Today, Hershey is a very _____
    PLURAL NOUN   ADJECTIVE

place. There are _____ roller coasters there, and the fastest one
     NUMBER

travels at seventy-five _____ per hour. Just don't eat too
       PLURAL NOUN

many _____ before you board, or you'll be sorry!
 PLURAL NOUN

From WHO WAS? MAD LIBS® • Copyright © 2016 by Penguin Random House LLC.

MAD LIBS® is fun to play with friends, but you can also play it by yourself! To begin with, DO NOT look at the story on the page below. Fill in the blanks on this page with the words called for. Then, using the words you have selected, fill in the blank spaces in the story.

Now you've created your own hilarious MAD LIBS® game!

KING TUT: WELCOME TO MY PYRAMID

NUMBER _____

VERB (PAST TENSE) _____

ADJECTIVE _____

PLURAL NOUN _____

ADJECTIVE _____

PLURAL NOUN _____

PLURAL NOUN _____

ADJECTIVE _____

PLURAL NOUN _____

ANIMAL _____

PLURAL NOUN _____

TYPE OF LIQUID _____

NOUN _____

PLURAL NOUN _____

VERB (PAST TENSE) _____

ADJECTIVE _____

NOUN _____

MAD LIBS
KING TUT: WELCOME TO MY PYRAMID

Although I was only pharaoh for about _____ years and
NUMBER

_____ when I was still a teenager, my tomb was filled
VERB (PAST TENSE)

with many _____ _____. My _____
ADJECTIVE   PLURAL NOUN   ADJECTIVE

tomb had many _____ filled with _____ for
PLURAL NOUN   PLURAL NOUN

my time in the afterlife, including a/an _____ bed, gold
ADJECTIVE

_____, food, and my pet _____. Each of my
PLURAL NOUN   ANIMAL

_____ was put into a special jar along with sacred
PLURAL NOUN

_____ and labeled "_____," "liver," "intestines,"
TYPE OF LIQUID   NOUN

and "_____." My mummy was _____
PLURAL NOUN   VERB (PAST TENSE)

and placed inside a great _____ box called a/an _____.
ADJECTIVE   NOUN

MAD LIBS® is fun to play with friends, but you can also play it by yourself! To begin with, DO NOT look at the story on the page below. Fill in the blanks on this page with the words called for. Then, using the words you have selected, fill in the blank spaces in the story.

Now you've created your own hilarious MAD LIBS® game!

DA VINCI
(THE MAD LIBS CODE)

NOUN _____

LAST NAME _____

NOUN _____

ADJECTIVE _____

PART OF THE BODY _____

ARTICLE OF CLOTHING _____

ADJECTIVE _____

ADJECTIVE _____

PART OF THE BODY (PLURAL) _____

NOUN _____

FIRST NAME (FEMALE) _____

VERB (PAST TENSE) _____

NOUN _____

FIRST NAME (MALE) _____

A PLACE _____

NOUN _____

A PLACE _____

MAD LIBS®
DA VINCI
(THE MAD LIBS CODE)

The *Mona Lisa* is probably the most famous ___Hair___ in the
                                              NOUN

world. It was painted sometime between 1503 and 1517 by Leonardo

da ___Jones___, and the ___Hinzajoes___ in the painting has a
      LAST NAME   NOUN

very ___oily___ ___ear Loab___. What is her secret? Her
      ADJECTIVE   PART OF THE BODY

___sock___ is very ___stiky___. She wears no
ARTICLE OF CLOTHING   ADJECTIVE

___green___ jewelry. Her ___pinky+use___ appear to be
ADJECTIVE   PART OF THE BODY (PLURAL)

looking out at a/an ___Halbbordord___ that only she can see. We are not
                         NOUN

even sure that her name *was* actually ___mifa___! Leonardo
                                        FIRST NAME (FEMALE)

___swolld___ this painting very much. He kept it with him
VERB (PAST TENSE)

for the rest of his ___coshre saace___. When King ___Kony___ of
                         NOUN   FIRST NAME (MALE)

(the) ___Hongkong___ invited Leonardo to move to France, he brought
         A PLACE

the ___tea pot___ with him. Today it hangs in (the) ___The nearst bus stion___
       NOUN   A PLACE

in the famous Louvre Museum.

MAD LIBS® is fun to play with friends, but you can also play it by yourself! To begin with, DO NOT look at the story on the page below. Fill in the blanks on this page with the words called for. Then, using the words you have selected, fill in the blank spaces in the story.

Now you've created your own hilarious MAD LIBS® game!

QUOTH THE MAD LIBS: "NEVERMORE!"

ADJECTIVE _____

ADJECTIVE _____

ADJECTIVE _____

NOUN _____

NOUN _____

NOUN _____

NOUN _____

VERB _____

NOUN _____

NOUN _____

NOUN _____

PLURAL NOUN _____

FIRST NAME (FEMALE) _____

ADJECTIVE _____

PLURAL NOUN _____

ADJECTIVE _____

MAD LIBS
QUOTH THE MAD LIBS: "NEVERMORE!"

Once upon a midnight _____, while I pondered,
ADJECTIVE

_____ and weary,
ADJECTIVE

Over many a/an _____ and curious _____ of forgotten lore,
ADJECTIVE   NOUN

While I nodded, nearly napping, suddenly there came a tapping,

As of some one gently rapping, rapping at my chamber _____.
NOUN

"'Tis some _____," I muttered, "tapping at my chamber door—
NOUN

Only _____, and nothing more."
NOUN

Ah, distinctly I _____ it was in the bleak December,
VERB

And each separate dying _____ wrought its ghost upon the
NOUN

_____.
NOUN

Eagerly I wished the _____—vainly I had sought to borrow
NOUN

From my _____ surcease of sorrow—sorrow for the lost
PLURAL NOUN

_____—
FIRST NAME (FEMALE)

For the rare and _____ maiden whom the _____ name
ADJECTIVE   PLURAL NOUN

Lenore—

_____ here for evermore.
ADJECTIVE

From WHO WAS? MAD LIBS® • Copyright © 2016 by Penguin Random House LLC.

MAD LIBS® is fun to play with friends, but you can also play it by yourself! To begin with, DO NOT look at the story on the page below. Fill in the blanks on this page with the words called for. Then, using the words you have selected, fill in the blank spaces in the story.

Now you've created your own hilarious MAD LIBS® game!

WHAT DOES YOUR FAVORITE AUTHOR SAY ABOUT YOU?

PLURAL NOUN _____

VERB _____

ADJECTIVE _____

ADJECTIVE _____

PLURAL NOUN _____

TYPE OF FOOD _____

ADJECTIVE _____

NOUN _____

NOUN _____

PLURAL NOUN _____

NOUN _____

COLOR _____

ANIMAL _____

ADJECTIVE _____

NOUN _____

NOUN _____

MAD LIBS
WHAT DOES YOUR FAVORITE
AUTHOR SAY ABOUT YOU?

- If you love wizards, potions, and _____, J. K. Rowling

PLURAL NOUN

  is the author for you! Your imagination will _____ you

VERB

  to _____ faraway places! **You are a geek!**

ADJECTIVE

- If bunny rabbits make you _____, then you probably

ADJECTIVE

  enjoy the books of Beatrix Potter. Talking _____

PLURAL NOUN

  who eat _____ from the garden patch would

TYPE OF FOOD

  make _____ BFFs. **You are an animal lover!**

ADJECTIVE

- If you can rhyme _____ and _____ with *cat* and

NOUN   NOUN

  hat, and you love silly words and even sillier _____,

PLURAL NOUN

  then you are most likely a Dr. Seuss _____! **You are a**

NOUN

  fan of _____ **eggs and ham!**

COLOR

- If you enjoy wearing a/an _____ costume and making

ANIMAL

  a/an _____ mess of things around your _____,

ADJECTIVE   NOUN

  then Maurice Sendak might be the _____ for you! **You**

NOUN

  are a wild thing!

MAD LIBS® is fun to play with friends, but you can also play it by yourself! To begin with, DO NOT look at the story on the page below. Fill in the blanks on this page with the words called for. Then, using the words you have selected, fill in the blank spaces in the story.

Now you've created your own hilarious MAD LIBS® game!

THE MEN IN STONE: MOUNT RUSHMORE

ADJECTIVE _____

NUMBER _____

NOUN _____

FIRST NAME (MALE) _____

NOUN _____

VERB (PAST TENSE) _____

NOUN _____

NOUN _____

ADJECTIVE _____

FIRST NAME (MALE) _____

PART OF THE BODY (PLURAL) _____

NUMBER _____

PART OF THE BODY _____

ADJECTIVE _____

PLURAL NOUN _____

VERB _____

ADJECTIVE _____

NOUN _____

MAD LIBS
THE MEN IN STONE: MOUNT RUSHMORE

Mount Rushmore is one of the world's most _____ sculptures!
                                              ADJECTIVE

The _____ men carved on the face of the _____
       NUMBER   NOUN

represent the first 150 years of American history. They are:

_____ Washington, the _____ of our country;
FIRST NAME (MALE)   NOUN

Thomas Jefferson, who _____ the Declaration of
                          VERB (PAST TENSE)

_____; Abraham Lincoln, who united the _____
     NOUN   NOUN

during the _____ War; and _____ Roosevelt,
              ADJECTIVE   FIRST NAME (MALE)

who people said looked very much like the sculptor! The

_____ of the presidents are amazing. Each eye is
PART OF THE BODY (PLURAL)

_____ feet wide! Each _____ is twenty feet long! Every
   NUMBER   PART OF THE BODY

year, the _____ Park Service inspects the carving for
              ADJECTIVE

_____. They work hard to _____ any cracks on
  PLURAL NOUN   VERB

this _____ national monument. Make sure you add a visit to
        ADJECTIVE

this incredible monument to your _____ list!
                                      NOUN

MAD LIBS® is fun to play with friends, but you can also play it by yourself! To begin with, DO NOT look at the story on the page below. Fill in the blanks on this page with the words called for. Then, using the words you have selected, fill in the blank spaces in the story.

Now you've created your own hilarious MAD LIBS® game!

WRITERS OF THE VICTORIAN ERA

A PLACE _____

NUMBER _____

ADJECTIVE _____

NOUN _____

NOUN _____

ADJECTIVE _____

ADJECTIVE _____

ADJECTIVE _____

PLURAL NOUN _____

NUMBER _____

NOUN _____

ADJECTIVE _____

OCCUPATION _____

PLURAL NOUN _____

NOUN _____

NOUN _____

A PLACE _____

ADJECTIVE _____

MAD LIBS
WRITERS OF THE VICTORIAN ERA

Queen Victoria became queen of (the) _____ when she was
_____ A PLACE

only _____ years old. Her long and _____ reign became
_____ NUMBER _____ ADJECTIVE

known as the Victorian _____. She sat on the _____
_____ NOUN _____ NOUN

for over sixty years. During that time, the most _____ author
_____ ADJECTIVE

in the world was Charles Dickens. Dickens wrote hundreds of

_____ stories and fifteen novels. Some of his most
ADJECTIVE

_____ titles are *Great* _____, *A Tale of* _____
ADJECTIVE _____ PLURAL NOUN _____ NUMBER

Cities, and *A Christmas* _____. During this same time, in the
_____ NOUN

United States, Mark Twain was quickly becoming America's most

_____ _____. He wrote *The* _____ *of*
ADJECTIVE OCCUPATION _____ PLURAL NOUN

Tom Sawyer and *A Connecticut* _____ *in King Arthur's*
_____ NOUN

_____. What are you waiting for? Head to your local
NOUN

_____ and pick up a novel by one of these _____
A PLACE _____ ADJECTIVE

authors. You won't be sorry!

MAD LIBS® is fun to play with friends, but you can also play it by yourself! To begin with, DO NOT look at the story on the page below. Fill in the blanks on this page with the words called for. Then, using the words you have selected, fill in the blank spaces in the story.

Now you've created your own hilarious MAD LIBS® game!

THE ADAMS FAMILY

ADJECTIVE _____

NOUN _____

NOUN _____

PLURAL NOUN _____

PLURAL NOUN _____

PLURAL NOUN _____

OCCUPATION _____

FIRST NAME (MALE) _____

VERB _____

A PLACE _____

NOUN _____

PLURAL NOUN _____

OCCUPATION _____

MAD LIBS

THE ADAMS FAMILY

The Adams family is one of the most _____ families in US
                                        ADJECTIVE
history, and they have Abigail Adams to thank for it. Abigail was both

the wife of a/an _____, John Adams, and the _____
                      NOUN   NOUN
of a president, John Quincy Adams. Abigail's _____ didn't
                                                PLURAL NOUN
think John Adams was good enough for her because he came from a

family of _____. Abigail loved to write _____
          PLURAL NOUN   PLURAL NOUN
full of news to her husband, _____ _____. She
                                OCCUPATION   FIRST NAME (MALE)
was the original First Lady to _____ in (the) _____.
                                  VERB   A PLACE
When she first visited Washington, DC, she declared, "It is the dirtiest

_____ I ever saw!" Six _____ after Abigail died,
    NOUN   PLURAL NOUN
her son, John Quincy Adams, became the sixth _____ of the
                                                OCCUPATION
United States.

MAD LIBS® is fun to play with friends, but you can also play it by yourself! To begin with, DO NOT look at the story on the page below. Fill in the blanks on this page with the words called for. Then, using the words you have selected, fill in the blank spaces in the story.

Now you've created your own hilarious MAD LIBS® game!

CAMPING WITH HENRY FORD AND THOMAS EDISON

ADJECTIVE _____

PLURAL NOUN _____

NOUN _____

ADJECTIVE _____

VERB _____

ADJECTIVE _____

ADJECTIVE _____

VERB _____

OCCUPATION (PLURAL) _____

VERB _____

ADJECTIVE _____

PLURAL NOUN _____

ANIMAL (PLURAL) _____

ADJECTIVE _____

VERB _____

NOUN _____

MAD LIBS®
CAMPING WITH HENRY FORD
AND THOMAS EDISON

Thomas: "I love spending time in the _____ outdoors,
ADJECTIVE

climbing _____, and acting like a/an _____ at
PLURAL NOUN   NOUN

summer camp!"

Henry: "Yes, but thank goodness I invented a/an _____ truck
ADJECTIVE

with a kitchen so that we can _____ a few _____
VERB   ADJECTIVE

meals out here!"

Thomas: "True, but we've been all over New England and the Great

_____ Mountains, and we still don't _____ any
ADJECTIVE   VERB

electricity!"

Henry: "Don't worry. We brought plenty of _____ to
OCCUPATION (PLURAL)

_____ our dinners and pitch our tents."
VERB

Thomas: "You're right. We're just two _____ inventors
ADJECTIVE

chopping _____ and fishing for _____,
PLURAL NOUN   ANIMAL (PLURAL)

while our servants and the _____ reporters _____ us
ADJECTIVE   VERB

through the woods. What a/an _____!"
NOUN

MAD LIBS® is fun to play with friends, but you can also play it by yourself! To begin with, DO NOT look at the story on the page below. Fill in the blanks on this page with the words called for. Then, using the words you have selected, fill in the blank spaces in the story.

Now you've created your own hilarious MAD LIBS® game!

TIPS FOR THE
SPACE TRAVELER

ADJECTIVE _____

NUMBER _____

TYPE OF FOOD _____

OCCUPATION (PLURAL) _____

PLURAL NOUN _____

ADJECTIVE _____

PLURAL NOUN _____

ADJECTIVE _____

VERB _____

PLURAL NOUN _____

VERB _____

ADJECTIVE _____

VERB _____

PART OF THE BODY _____

ADJECTIVE _____

TYPE OF FOOD _____

MAD LIBS®
TIPS FOR THE
SPACE TRAVELER

Neil Armstrong's tips:

1. Always have a/an _____ breakfast before blasting off.
   _{ADJECTIVE}

   The *Apollo* _____ crew had _____ and eggs—the
   _{NUMBER}   _{TYPE OF FOOD}

   same breakfast all _____ have before a flight.
   _{OCCUPATION (PLURAL)}

2. Don't spend more than two _____ on the surface of
   _{PLURAL NOUN}

   the moon. You won't have a/an _____ supply of oxygen
   _{ADJECTIVE}

   in your _____.
   _{PLURAL NOUN}

3. Collect plenty of _____ rocks, and _____
   _{ADJECTIVE}   _{VERB}

   pictures so you can prove to your _____ that you
   _{PLURAL NOUN}

   made it to the moon!

Sally Ride's tips:

1. Be prepared! Learn to _____ out of planes and scuba
   _{VERB}

   dive in _____ water. You have to _____ many
   _{ADJECTIVE}   _{VERB}

   survival skills.

2. Learn to catch a floating cookie with your _____!
   _{PART OF THE BODY}

3. Keep the space shuttle _____! Even a small bit of
   _{ADJECTIVE}

   _____ can clog up the computers on board.
   _{TYPE OF FOOD}

From WHO WAS? MAD LIBS® • Copyright © 2016 by Penguin Random House LLC.

MAD LIBS® is fun to play with friends, but you can also play it by yourself! To begin with, DO NOT look at the story on the page below. Fill in the blanks on this page with the words called for. Then, using the words you have selected, fill in the blank spaces in the story.

Now you've created your own hilarious MAD LIBS® game!

FRIDA KAHLO
AND PABLO PICASSO

ADJECTIVE _____

NOUN _____

ADJECTIVE _____

ADJECTIVE _____

NOUN _____

SILLY WORD _____

ADJECTIVE _____

A PLACE _____

ADJECTIVE _____

OCCUPATION _____

COLOR _____

NOUN _____

SILLY WORD _____

PLURAL NOUN _____

ADJECTIVE _____

PLURAL NOUN _____

PLURAL NOUN _____

Frida Kahlo was a/an _____, Mexican _____. She
ADJECTIVE NOUN
was famous for dressing in _____ clothing and for her
ADJECTIVE
_____ self-portraits. Her _____ style was known as
ADJECTIVE NOUN
_____-ism.
SILLY WORD

Pablo Picasso was the most _____ artist of the twentieth
ADJECTIVE
century. He was born in (the) _____ in 1881. Pablo is
A PLACE
considered the first _____ _____. He is known for
ADJECTIVE OCCUPATION
his _____ period, _____-ism, and even
COLOR NOUN
_____-ism, like Frida Kahlo. He had many famous
SILLY WORD
_____.
PLURAL NOUN

Pablo once gave Frida a/an _____ gift—a pair of
ADJECTIVE
_____ shaped like _____.
PLURAL NOUN PLURAL NOUN

MAD LIBS® is fun to play with friends, but you can also play it by yourself! To begin with, DO NOT look at the story on the page below. Fill in the blanks on this page with the words called for. Then, using the words you have selected, fill in the blank spaces in the story.

Now you've created your own hilarious MAD LIBS® game!

BLACKBEARD (THE MOST FEARED MAD LIBS)

NOUN _____

NOUN _____

ADVERB _____

NOUN _____

ADJECTIVE _____

PLURAL NOUN _____

PLURAL NOUN _____

NOUN _____

PART OF THE BODY _____

NOUN _____

PLURAL NOUN _____

ADJECTIVE _____

NUMBER _____

PLURAL NOUN _____

PART OF THE BODY _____

ADJECTIVE _____

NOUN _____

MAD LIBS®
BLACKBEARD (THE MOST FEARED MAD LIBS)

The early 1700s are considered the "Golden _____ of Piracy."
                                              NOUN

Pirates voted one _____ as captain. They shared their treasure
                     NOUN

_____. And they did not follow the rules of the
   ADVERB

_____ or any government. Some pirates were known for their
   NOUN

_____, fancy clothes and the _____ they
  ADJECTIVE   PLURAL NOUN

plundered, like rum, _____, gold, _____, and
                        PLURAL NOUN   NOUN

silver. Blackbeard, on the other _____, was famous for his
                                   PART OF THE BODY

long, black _____. He frightened _____ from the
              NOUN   PLURAL NOUN

American colonies to the _____ Sea. Blackbeard was killed by
                            ADJECTIVE

being shot _____ times and slashed twenty times with
              NUMBER

_____. And then his _____ was cut off. It took a
  PLURAL NOUN   PART OF THE BODY

lot to kill Blackbeard. After all, he was the most _____
                                                       ADJECTIVE

_____ of all time!
   NOUN

MAD LIBS® is fun to play with friends, but you can also play it by yourself! To begin with, DO NOT look at the story on the page below. Fill in the blanks on this page with the words called for. Then, using the words you have selected, fill in the blank spaces in the story.

Now you've created your own hilarious MAD LIBS® game!

FRIENDS OF THE WILD, WILD WEST

ADJECTIVE _____

PLURAL NOUN _____

OCCUPATION _____

ADJECTIVE _____

VERB _____

NOUN _____

ADJECTIVE _____

ANIMAL _____

PLURAL NOUN _____

ADJECTIVE _____

PLURAL NOUN _____

ADJECTIVE _____

NOUN _____

NOUN _____

ADJECTIVE _____

A PLACE _____

Buffalo Bill Cody ran a/an _____ show he called the Wild
<u>ADJECTIVE</u>

West. Two of its biggest _____ were Annie Oakley and
<u>PLURAL NOUN</u>

Sitting Bull, _____ of the Lakota Sioux. Annie was a/an
<u>OCCUPATION</u>

_____ woman who could _____ just about any
<u>ADJECTIVE</u>   <u>VERB</u>

_____. Sitting Bull called her "Little _____ Shot."
<u>NOUN</u>   <u>ADJECTIVE</u>

They were both excellent _____-back riders. The two
<u>ANIMAL</u>

_____ became _____ friends. Sitting Bull gave Annie
<u>PLURAL NOUN</u>   <u>ADJECTIVE</u>

many _____, including his moccasins from the Battle of the
<u>PLURAL NOUN</u>

_____ Bighorn. He admired her skill with a/an _____
<u>ADJECTIVE</u>   <u>NOUN</u>

and even adopted her as his _____! They both became
<u>NOUN</u>

symbols of the _____ West, even though Annie had never
<u>ADJECTIVE</u>

traveled west of (the) _____!
<u>A PLACE</u>

MAD LIBS® is fun to play with friends, but you can also play it by yourself! To begin with, DO NOT look at the story on the page below. Fill in the blanks on this page with the words called for. Then, using the words you have selected, fill in the blank spaces in the story.

Now you've created your own hilarious MAD LIBS® game!

THE GREATEST!

ADJECTIVE _____

VERB _____

NOUN _____

ADJECTIVE _____

ADJECTIVE _____

PLURAL NOUN _____

ANIMAL _____

VERB _____

PART OF THE BODY (PLURAL) _____

VERB _____

PART OF THE BODY (PLURAL) _____

FIRST NAME (MALE) _____

VERB (PAST TENSE) _____

ANIMAL _____

VERB (PAST TENSE) _____

NOUN _____

VERB ENDING IN "ING" _____

MAD LIBS

THE GREATEST!

There's no question that Muhammad Ali was one of the most

_____ boxers of all time. However, he never liked to
   ADJECTIVE

_____ about his skills in the _____. He was always
   VERB   NOUN

_____, _____, and proud. One of his most well-known
  ADJECTIVE   ADJECTIVE

_____ is "Float like a/an _____, _____
 PLURAL NOUN   ANIMAL   VERB

like a bee. The _____ can't _____
               PART OF THE BODY (PLURAL)   VERB

what the _____ can't see." And in 1974, before
         PART OF THE BODY (PLURAL)

fighting _____ Foreman in Zaire, he said, "I have
     FIRST NAME (MALE)

_____ with an alligator, I have tussled with a/an
 VERB (PAST TENSE)

_____. I have _____ lightning, and put
   ANIMAL   VERB (PAST TENSE)

_____ in jail." It's not _____ if you can back it up.
  NOUN   VERB ENDING IN "ING"

MAD LIBS® is fun to play with friends, but you can also play it by yourself! To begin with, DO NOT look at the story on the page below. Fill in the blanks on this page with the words called for. Then, using the words you have selected, fill in the blank spaces in the story.

Now you've created your own hilarious MAD LIBS® game!

HOUND DOG
OR DON GIOVANNI?

ADJECTIVE _____

ADVERB _____

PLURAL NOUN _____

VERB (PAST TENSE) _____

NOUN _____

PLURAL NOUN _____

VERB (PAST TENSE) _____

PLURAL NOUN _____

ADJECTIVE _____

ADJECTIVE _____

PLURAL NOUN _____

ADJECTIVE _____

VEHICLE _____

ADJECTIVE _____

VERB (PAST TENSE) _____

Did you know that Elvis and Mozart had a lot in common? They both

discovered music at a very _____ age. And they both worked
ADJECTIVE

_____ hard at it! Both Elvis and Mozart performed to earn
ADVERB

_____ to give to their families. They both
PLURAL NOUN

_____ all night and often went to _____ at
VERB (PAST TENSE)   NOUN

dawn. In the eighteenth century, Mozart wrote operas which

were like the Las Vegas _____ of their time. Elvis
PLURAL NOUN

_____ in Las Vegas. Both men performed in fancy,
VERB (PAST TENSE)

embroidered _____ and costumes. They loved wearing
PLURAL NOUN

_____ clothes and throwing _____ parties for all
ADJECTIVE   ADJECTIVE

their _____. Mozart had his _____ coach, and
PLURAL NOUN   ADJECTIVE

Elvis drove a/an _____. Both Elvis and Mozart met their
VEHICLE

_____ wives in Germany. And they both _____
ADJECTIVE   VERB (PAST TENSE)

too young—Mozart at thirty-five, and Elvis at age forty-two. Which

one is your favorite: Mozart or Elvis?

MAD LIBS® is fun to play with friends, but you can also play it by yourself! To begin with, DO NOT look at the story on the page below. Fill in the blanks on this page with the words called for. Then, using the words you have selected, fill in the blank spaces in the story.

Now you've created your own hilarious MAD LIBS® game!

THE BRAINIAC'S MAD LIBS

ADJECTIVE _____

VERB _____

PLURAL NOUN _____

PLURAL NOUN _____

ADJECTIVE _____

PLURAL NOUN _____

PLURAL NOUN _____

VERB _____

OCCUPATION _____

ADVERB _____

LETTER OF THE ALPHABET _____

ADJECTIVE _____

PART OF THE BODY _____

NOUN _____

VERB ENDING IN "S" _____

A PLACE _____

Albert Einstein was a/an _____, shy, and quiet boy. He loved
__ADJECTIVE__

to just sit and _____. Albert thought there was real power in
__VERB__

_____. He even said that the imagination is more important
__PLURAL NOUN__

than _____. Electricity amazed Albert because it was
__PLURAL NOUN__

_____, powerful, and dangerous. And he liked mysterious
__ADJECTIVE__

_____. School didn't always teach Albert the
__PLURAL NOUN__

_____ he wanted to know about, so he began to
__PLURAL NOUN__

_____ himself. Some kids dream about becoming a/an
__VERB__

_____, but Albert knew he would grow up to be a thinker.
__OCCUPATION__

And he was a/an _____ original thinker! His most famous
__ADVERB__

equation is _____$=mc^2$. Albert was one of the most
__LETTER OF THE ALPHABET__

_____ scientists who ever lived. After he died, his
__ADJECTIVE__

_____ was donated to science. For years, it was kept in a/an
__PART OF THE BODY__

_____ marked "cider." Einstein's brain now_____
__NOUN__   __VERB ENDING IN "S"__

in a jar in (the) _____, New Jersey.
__A PLACE__

MAD LIBS® is fun to play with friends, but you can also play it by yourself! To begin with, DO NOT look at the story on the page below. Fill in the blanks on this page with the words called for. Then, using the words you have selected, fill in the blank spaces in the story.

Now you've created your own hilarious MAD LIBS® game!

THE GREAT ESCAPE: HARRY HOUDINI

OCCUPATION _____

NOUN _____

NOUN _____

ANIMAL _____

NOUN _____

VERB _____

ADJECTIVE _____

VERB _____

PLURAL NOUN _____

OCCUPATION _____

PLURAL NOUN _____

PLURAL NOUN _____

VERB ENDING IN "ING" _____

PLURAL NOUN _____

MAD◉LIBS®
THE GREAT ESCAPE:
HARRY HOUDINI

I was a/an _____ who could escape from any _____,
       OCCUPATION   NOUN

handcuffs, or _____. I became well-known for making a huge
                NOUN

_____ disappear on the _____ during one of my
    ANIMAL   NOUN

acts. I even appeared to be able to _____ through a/an
                                      VERB

_____ wall! But my real hobby was exposing people who
 ADJECTIVE

believed they could _____ with the _____ of the
                     VERB   PLURAL NOUN

dead. I learned all their tricks. I even wrote a book called *A/An*

_____ *Among the* _____. When I wasn't busy
  OCCUPATION   PLURAL NOUN

with my stage and screen _____, I spent time
                               PLURAL NOUN

_____ fake _____.
VERB ENDING IN "ING"   PLURAL NOUN

MAD LIBS® is fun to play with friends, but you can also play it by yourself! To begin with, DO NOT look at the story on the page below. Fill in the blanks on this page with the words called for. Then, using the words you have selected, fill in the blank spaces in the story.

Now you've created your own hilarious MAD LIBS® game!

THE FAST AND THE FURIOUS

NOUN _____

NUMBER _____

NOUN _____

NOUN _____

VERB _____

ADJECTIVE _____

NOUN _____

A PLACE _____

NOUN _____

COLOR _____

PART OF THE BODY _____

NOUN _____

ANIMAL (PLURAL) _____

TYPE OF LIQUID _____

ADJECTIVE _____

NOUN _____

ADVERB _____

ADJECTIVE _____

THE FAST AND THE FURIOUS

Super sprinter Jesse Owens was known as "the fastest _____
NOUN

in the world." On a single day in 1933, he equalled a world record and

set _____ national high-school records. In 1935, he had another
NUMBER

record-winning _____—tying a world _____ in the
NOUN   NOUN

100-yard _____ and shattering the record for the
VERB

_____ jump. The 1936 _____ Olympics were held
ADJECTIVE   NOUN

in Berlin, _____. Jesse Owens became the first American
A PLACE

_____ to ever win four track-and-field _____ medals
NOUN   COLOR

at the Olympic Games.

On the other _____, Genghis Khan was the feared ruler of
PART OF THE BODY

the largest _____ empire in history. As a boy, he hunted
NOUN

_____ to survive. He built catapults to hurl vats of
ANIMAL (PLURAL)

_____ at his enemies. He even killed his own _____
TYPE OF LIQUID   ADJECTIVE

brother with a bow and _____!
NOUN

Jesse Owens and Genghis Khan: _____ fast, too
ADVERB

_____.
ADJECTIVE